The Dude 'du Jour' of Somalia

Eli Shaber

GREENPOINT PRESS
NEW YORK, NY

ISBN 978-0-9832370-9-9

Library of Congress Cataloging-in-Publication Data

This edition designed by David Chang
Text and Heads set in Quadraat Sans Pro

Greenpoint Press,
a division of New York Writers Resources
PO Box 2062
Lenox Hill Station
New York, NY 10021

New York Writers Resources:
newyorkwritersresources.com
newyorkwritersworkshop.com
greenpointpress.org
ducts.org

Printed in the United States
on acid-free paper

DR. Z

So I get this call around 9 o'clock
On a Friday night

Don't usually pick-up the phone that late

But, ya know
I had a feeling

It's a guy I've known forever

The first person I ever lived with outside of my parents' home
My ancient college roommate

Goes by the name of Dr. Z

Says we gotta meet for coffee
8:30 in the morning

Eighty-sixth and Columbus

Must be important

He's a man of extraordinary talent
At the top of his field

World class, for sure

Three heart attacks later
And a daily fistful of digitalis

Nothin' slows this dinosaur down

His heart is filled to capacity
With near toxic levels of love

Tells me he's in a terrible jam
Going on a mercy mission to Somalia

Probably his toughest trick ever

Needs a surgeon
Yesterday

His steady 'boy' can't leave the country
Intensive Care

I know where this discussion is headed
And I'm gettin' justifiably nervous

I've been retired for a while now
Pretty much outta the loop

Why not take a shot, he musta figured
I guess anyone with a pulse was worth asking

He leaned in
Extra close

And inquired

"Do you have the balls to drop everything in your life"

To do the Good work
The Big work

Ya never know
It might change your outlook

Just so happens
What I needed most in my life was somethin' large

Been some tough sludgin' in the old man's head
For quite a while now

My longest bummer ever

Shhh, quiet
Listen carefully

Can ya hear it
It's elusive

That knocking sound

That, my friend, is Mr. Opportunity
And I'm his catch of the day

Slow down, Doc
Tempo

Gotta clear it with the ball and chain

Long story short

Went home
Told my old lady

She looked me square in the eye

"Make me proud, Papa"
"Be a show stopper"

Case Closed

Grabbed a downtown 'C' local

Got a visa

I'm outta here

OPENING ACT

The car service is about to arrive
Twenty minutes or so

My pulse is jammin'
My chest feels tight

Haven't felt this way since the Surgical Boards in Chicago
Over forty years ago

Hard to believe it's been just six days
Six delirious days

Since being chosen for this mission

I've been furiously obsessing about traveling light
'De rigueur'

Allowed only two rolls of toilet paper
A smattering of food

No change of clothes
Just necessary meds

Some kinda' happy horse shit about Jeeps and weight distribution

Luckily, my dear friend Michael set me straight

"You're being way too literal, Man"

What if ya bring extra stuff
What are they gonna do

Send ya home

Thanks Mike
It made all the difference

I decided to go for a human touch

Bought a Boom-Box
And 24 'D' batteries

Ya know, the big ones

Just doubled my weight

Hopped in a cab
Headed Uptown

Picked up a box of Davidoff Cigars
Lansford Blunts

Clean draw
Great flavor

Chic as hell

Hey, Honey-Honey
Remind me to get some of those fancy lollipops I like so much

"I Can Resist Anything But Temptation"

I'm at the airport
Passing customs

I must have the look of a lunatic

The TSA attacked my luggage like a swarm of locusts
Tearing through a Whole Foods

They searched my nostrils

Flight called
Gate 12D

Ladies and Gentleman
We are pleased to announce the departure of Flight #743

Direct
To Kenya

Oh Baby, I can make one hell of a case for God
Based merely on the fact that Business Class exists

BIG SECURITY

Meet my partner in Nairobi
5:30 am

Dr. Z is in town

Get in a U.N. truck
Big security

Two U.S. Marines
Armed to the teeth

They're the size of Hummers

They never spoke a word
Not one word

Our driver, Joseph, is beside himself
Can't believe his good fortune

His very own military escort
Could his day possibly get any better

I give him a killer lollipop

'Alhamdulillah'

KYAT

Just so ya know

There's a huge problem in Kenya with marauding gangs

Stone cold thugs
Sporting some seriously unpleasant vendettas

The locals call them bandits

Bandits, my ass

I got nothin' to fear
Not with these monsters in the truck

The ride is about ten hours
My left kidney exploded at hour eight

We stop in Garissa
A small, slimy way station on the way to Dertu

Scored some Kyat from a Black 'black market' Gangsta

Kyat
It's like cocoa leaf or beetle nut

Nasty, nasty taste
Edgy, like a razor

One serious macho buzz

"A Day Without A Buzz Is Like A Day That Never Was"

Blistering, sweltering heat
Hottest day of the year in Kenya

Arrive in Dertu
Late

It's as dark as the other side of the moon

Joseph still hasn't finished his lolly
The thing's been in his mouth for at least eight hours

Strange, No?

In my current state of unhinged discombobulation
Somehow this augurs poorly

Ah, why make a megillah
Maybe the guy's just eccentric

INDIANA

I'm given a tour of my accommodations

One mattress

Previously discarded
Subsequently resurrected

Something a beggar from Mumbai would put over a grate

Pure 'Dada'

The heat is relentless
Nevertheless, we sleep with tightly tucked blankets

Rats and mice and scorpions
Oh my

Thank goodness the flies and mosquitoes have the sense to leave this place

Day 2

Arise early
Took a cold shower

It's the only cold anything I'll feel for the next eight days

Can't use any of my food
No boiling water

My coffee and oatmeal are as useful to me as a 'sky-hook'

Put on my scrub suit
Lit a stogie

Feeling all cool
And humanitarian

Indeed, a real 'Indiana Cohens'

Off across the border to the Somali refugee camp
The place has no name

Have to walk quite a distance
Never felt heat like this so early in the morning

Gotta make this schlep four times a day

No food, no coffee
Mega-hungry

A canary in a coal mine

My head feels like that crazy scene from 'Reservoir Dogs'

"Clowns To the Left Of Me"
"Jokers to the Right"

"Here I Am"
Stuck

Damn, where's that Vicodin when you need it for real

Menacing cloud ahead
Thick as porridge

Hordes of people

The requisite carcass or two
Goat, cow, camel

Motha' fucking vultures
Everywhere

'The Horror'
'The Horror'

This definitely does not smell like Napalm in the morning

I feel like a complete, confused, quixotic impostor
A jerk-off poseur

All bets are off
It's official

This party is over

Time to go to war
And war it was

WIIL WAAL

Finally, the hospital doors open

The line wriggles into the desert
Far as I can see

'Registration time'

The first few patients begin to trickle into the clinic

Or, as I prefer call it
The 'Hold-the-Mayo' Clinic

Today was the first and last time I would ever see Wiil Waal
The three-legged kid

Has one regulation, league-sanctioned leg
Pretty damn nimble at that

One ugly-ass walking stick

And this other thing

A hideously withered, weeping stump
With a vestigial foot dangling uselessly off its working end

Was bitten by one of those killer desert snakes

Oh, This is sensational
Really rich

Killer-Desert-Snakes

I think I missed that class

Utterly flummoxed and breathtakingly out of my element

I go into my best, well honed
Doctor 'Doggy Paddle' routine

Where are the parents
'Dead'

Where is the family
'Dead'

Obviously, this approach is not recommended
Definitely not what I had intended

The conversation has now descended
To the point where I've clearly offended

Virtually every person in this shack

And, to make matters infinitely worse
The group insistently insists that I treat the boy here

Here
In this ramshackle lean-to

"Are You Out Of Your Fucking Mind"

Not today
Not tomorrow

Not ever

Not unless some 'Amputation Fairy' magically appears from under a pillow
Like in some 'Cirque du Soleil' extravaganza

I take an unfathomably deep breath

First I study the funky leg
It's lookin' angrier by the minute

Next, I check out funky leg's owner
Tough kid, strong kid

The situation is dicey and dire
Need to stretch a few never-to-be-stretched edicts

Find Joseph
"Tell him to bring the truck"

Gotta get Wiil Waal to Nairobi

"I'll pick up the tab"

Heard he died in transit

The story made the front page of the New York Times
Above the fold

I get the sweats when I'm reminded of it
Like a chronic pneumonia-addled nightmare

A never healing scab
Begging to be picked

BRUTES

We had some hot shot surgeons in from Nairobi
Here to lighten the load

Everybody knows
Charity starts at home

Not so fast cowpoke
All hat, no cattle

Strictly sizzle

I find myself in the company of
Privileged, elitist, contumacious, megalomaniacal sons-of-bitches

They strolled around
All straight and starched

I thought they were on their way to a fraternity party

Assiduously perusing the landscape
I carefully watch the 'Sigma Phi's' operate

Brutes

Over-schooled
Under-educated

Their hands
As soft as bricks

These guys handle delicate human tissue
As if it were disposable

They seem far more interested in clowning around

Like puerile bullies
In a sandbox

I am concretized

Where's the protocol
The surgical technique

For Christ's sake
Where's the humanity

Jethro, Peter, Mohammad

Goddamn it
Step-up

Show me that this matters

It's apparent
Right in front of your nose

These people are battered and bankrupt
Abandoned and abused

Off-the-hook invisible

Listen up

It's a fine, blurry, complex line between Tribal Leader and Mighty Whitey
Hard to get your head around at first

A real tight-rope walk
No net

Tough Shit

I got no time to await instructions

I came here on my own dime
To do business

Stay cool, flaco
Pay attention, old man

Always, tempo

The story is as old as dirt
It's about raw power

I'm certain I'll suss this scene out soon enough

This is like a hanging curveball
Right in my wheelhouse

After thirty years of hospital warfare
I can do raw power in my sleep

Decision Time
Decision Made

Just That Simple

No one, but no one
Is going to suffer needlessly on my watch

What's the point
It took me forty seven hours to get here

UM-MM

The majordomo leader of these egregious douche bags
Keeps shooting me looks

Ya know
Ugly glares

Even his lip curls

Yo, Ahmed

I snapped
And summoned him with my fingers

"Didn't you get the memo", Busta
This is my movie

Our eyes locked solid
It felt atavistic

Colossal

Um-mm
Like a dog in heat

I walk deliberately toward him
Omni-present Davidoff in my mouth

Total unabated eye contact
I got right in his grill

Took the rope out of my mouth

Blew a steady, hot stream of expensive smoke
Straight into his face

Told him if he stares at me again
I'll make his next eight days a living nightmare

That solipsistic 'jive-ass' bastard never looked my way again

"Pussy"

I'm the most hated man at the staff camp
Detested, really

With some luck and solid planning
I'll be despised by Thursday

They threaten mass mutiny

Go home
I don't give a fat rat's ass

Ever so reluctantly
They came to accept that this team has but one chief

Dr. Moi

Nevertheless, I'm still disinclined to cut these Brahman assholes a break

I make them ask for permission
To go to the toilet

Just between you and me

Now that this deal is sealed
And packed away

I really do regret that things didn't work out

Truth be told
I'm terribly disappointed

"This Bell Cannot Be Unrung"

TOO MUCH

Day 4

Torrential rain
Worked through it

Outside

Covered head to toe with thick red mud

Have to stop
This is getting nutty

"When There's Too Much, Something Is Missing"

Bam
Snap

Just like that

I get this great idea

Went into camp
Grabbed some boys

And the remnants of an old ball

'Game On'

Had two boys on either side of me
One in the center to hike

Hut 1
Hut 2

This rain is pounding, pelting, pounding

Hey you
I yelled

Yeah, you
You with the shaved head

Go deep to the giant termite hill
Turn around

I'll hit ya

The only words of spoken English these children will ever know

'Go Deep'

The rain stops as quickly as it started

Back to work

Within two hours the Earth is as dry as toast
And once again the Sun rules

At least I'm clean, dry and mud-less

I operated deep into that night
Chaperoned only by the nauseating fumes of a kerosene lamp

Atone, my son, atone

'Es Sabor Aqui'

I Dig It

ITTY-BITTY

Dinner served at 10 pm
Lunch at 3

Goat meat
Slaughtered daily by the villagers

Slow cooked in camel milk
With potato and carrot

Also, rice

A Somali delicacy

It oscillates between gritty and grisly
Goes down beautifully with a boiling hot Coca-Cola

Enormous platters of food

Family style
No utensils

We ate the same meal twice a day for eight days

I'd stick an ice pick through my ear for just one taste
One itty-bitty taste

Of Elizabeth's lasagna

QUÉ ONDA GUERO

Dr. Z runs this place like a M.A.S.H. unit
He's the camp's undefeated arm wrestler

A sixty-five year old Lantzman at that
Not even the 'Frito-Banditos' can take him down

He's a steamroller
A real mensch

Day 5

He takes me aside
Tells me straight up

"You gotta change up the scene"
"Find yourself a new routine"

The Brothers had this act on the road
For over 20 years

Up to two, three months at a pop

When 'Z' talks
I listen

Leave staff camp early
And venture over to the Somali salon

Escorted, as always, by my translator, Maurice

He pronounces it Morris

Oh, Maurice
My young African prodigy

Epicene and delicate
Like a spider's web

Ramrod solid

Tough
Like a tank

An unadulterated autodidact if ever there was one

Reminds me of Yoda
With industrial strength melanin

He re-acquaints me with the obvious

Whoa, Chief
"This is no place for a single 'O' white guy"

'Qué Onda Guero'

"A Coward Dies A Thousand Deaths"
"A Hero Dies But Once"

We went to meet a woman oddly enough named 'November'
In actuality she's a 14 year old girl

She made me breakfast every morning, henceforth

The menu is the same everyday

Chapati
Kinda like a thick greasy tortilla

Goat bone soup

And, of course
Sweet camel milk tea

I'm taught to sit properly, respectfully
It hurts my knees

I'M CURIOUS

After a couple of days of this so called 'venturing'

I began to assemble
A most diverse ensemble

'Bloomsbury Group'
African Style

A couple of U. N. truck drivers
Some local security guys

Even a thug or two is known to drop by

Things got pretty cozy and cushy at our breakfast soirees

So comfy, in fact
That I broached the unspoken

Sex, that is

Air out the laundry
Let out the beast

"I'm curious"
I asked, slyly

"When you make love with your women"
"Do you touch"

No way
They fervidly declared

Heads swiveling
Side-to-side

No words required

Maybe I've gone too far
Have I offended

Then again
Maybe not

From the corner of my eye
I caught a glimpse of Lansana and Runo

It's irrefutable
They were inquisitive

What do you mean
When you say 'touch'

Runo was down for the whole enchilada

Ya know
Kiss and Lick and Ya-Ya-Ya

"Lick"
"Lick What"

I pointed to their privates with my chin

They were flabbergasted

I sensed the perfect opportunity
And I seized it by the throat

Calmly
I set aside my chapati

Scrupulously cleansed my fingers

I gave the 'Thumbs-Up' sign

And then I Licked
And I Gnarled
And I Dawdled

At the tip of that big, fat, fleshy digit

I made it all wet and gooey
Just above the knuckle

Languid and Licentious

They seemed to be stupefied and mesmerized
Simultaneously

A child's first visit to the circus

"Think about it"
I suggested

Then
I gradually plunged my mouth down

Right down to the notch
Deep as I could

I swallowed the whole thing

Tasty, boys
Trust me

Super-duper tasty

They giggled like school girls at the junior prom

The only thing that was missing
Was the corsage

Went back to my bone soup as if nothing had been said

Just another banquet at November's 'Algonquin'

TEAR JERKER

I went into the kitchen to thank her

'Country French'
I think it was

I discretely slip her a 100 Kenyan Shilling Note
A buck thirty-two

Her knees began to tremble
I thought she might faint

This is beaucoup risky business
A white man alone with a totally veiled woman

She dropped her veil
Allowed me to see her face

Tears rolling from her eyes

She expects nothing from life
And that is precisely what she gets

I try with my last speck of testosterone not to cry

I'm afraid

Afraid if I start
I'll never be able to stop

No use
I match her tear for tear

Then, just for good measure
I raise her a few

The croupier was right
These dice are loaded

This was a moment

Rare and transcendental
Authentic and pure

Unamalgamated

It's the 'Uterine Lottery', Baby

Some win
Some lose

November lost

CHILL, DOC, CHILL

One cannot help but notice
Right outta the chute

Something is horribly amiss in Eden

There are no men here
None at all

Slaughtered and butchered
Butchered and slaughtered

Long gone

Yet, most bizarrely
Within this smorgasbord of hell and disease

Live some of the most stunningly beautiful woman
On the face of the planet

Black Ebony Angels

Steel hardened Muslims

Even the very youngest, enshrouded
Obligated, forever, to the veil

Rapacious poverty
Homeless and widowed

Always, poised and dignified

Their smiles are mesmeric
Clean and dazzling

Like a blizzard

Irony hovers over this place like a murky, rancid mist
The viscosity of crank-case oil

Maurice dumps a bottle of water over my dew rag

It's not meant as just a meaningless distraction
But, rather, a signal for me to regroup

Man, he's got me pegged
I must appear dazed or shell-shocked

Maybe I got one of those post-traumatic brain things

"Chill, Doc, Chill"

My protector and protégé
Implores me

In thick tribal dialect

"You've got to stop trying to make sense of this shit-hole"

That's cool, I nod

You're right, Mo
You're absolutely right

I most gently appease
This most gentle of men

I'm as disingenuous as the law will allow

I've lived long enough to know
Nothing short of a gigantic Quaalude is gonna handle this mess

My head is on fire
Feels like the last few hours of Yom Kippur

Same old mantra
Back to basics

Tempo, Papi
Glide

FLASHBACK

Been almost a week now
Living in the company of only men

Brings back long forgotten memories

Way back
Retro-back

Mid-sixties
Peace and Love and Re-vo-lu-tion

I was a soft and plump and buttery young man
My mother's baby boy

Had to buy my clothes at the Husky Shop
I still remember the sign

Wore my fraternity pin
Everyday, everywhere

Was proud to be livin' with the Brothers

I liked it then
I like it now

We live in a fenced-off, isolated, barbed-wired compound

Mockingly referred to as
'The Freedom Sanctuary'

Nice and quiet and effortless

No social amenities
No negotiations

We walk around in our underwear
Whenever we want

We piss wherever we choose

Everybody doin'
Their own private little dance

Over there in the corner
Mustafa, with some buddies

They're listening to the BBC

The radio is vintage World War One

An enormous turd
With static

Jethro hangs out by the latrine
Carries the Koran with him, always

Day and night
Sleeps with it

Never seen him crack the book or read a line
Religion by osmosis

He usually pals around with the Abdula
Quite possibly, the most important person in our secrete 'manclave'

He answers to the moniker
'Key Guy'

Abdula alone holds the keys to the Kingdom

No Key Guy
No water

INTERMEZZO

Apologies in advance

Gotta stop the 'con'
For just a second

Need to issue an urgent
'Cliché Alert'

Both my back and my heart are broken

I'm so embarrassed

I've never stood taller
I feel so small

It's full-out whacked here
How does shit like this keep happening

Human nature
Trenchant and murderous

And I get to witness it
In full grotesque bloom

Lemme tell ya
This is one tough gig

Body and spirit tested daily

This ridiculously ridiculous heat seems to have activated my access

Feels like I dropped half a tab
Of the 'Rainbow'

I can see it

Yeah
I see it clearly

My phylogeny, that is

Back in the day, they say
I was quite the wisenheimer

Things evolved, grew up a little
Got lucky

Became an all-timer

Life goes on
Now, I'm an old-timer

No doubt headed for the long vacation
With the Alzheimer

That's the way it rolls
Just connect the dots

My insignificance astounds even me
Obviously, still a work in progress

There are thousands of Dertus

Who cares
"I got my own aggravation"

Indulge me

Do not mistake my glib insouciance for insincerity

It's my armor
My shield

It's all I have left to protect me

Fact of the matter is
I'm subsumed

I think today is Tuesday
Maybe Wednesday

Can't be certain

Gotta be ready
Just in case

Today is a big day for me
A memorable day

I've been chosen to plant the first tree
At the site of a proposed school

A very special honor
I'm deeply humbled

I name my tree Jacob

Although I've never spent time in a war zone
I was never afraid for my safety

Peculiar really
Since I learned long ago

"Only Fools Are Fearless"

Not even the marauding punks bother me

Curiously enough
They can't seem to get enough of me

I'm the Dude 'du jour' in Somalia

PLOT TWIST

Against all odds
We copped a tang of unfettered joy

Just a pre-ordained, primordial pop-off
I suspect

I brought tunes from Al Green to ZZ Top
Even included some special cameos

The Rolling Uglies
Van the Man

And, of course
The Fab Four

A temporary peace flowered over the camp

Assisted quite nicely
Thank you

By that Kyat from Garissa

'Hosanna'
'Hosanna'

The sky is enormous tonight

And we danced

"It's A Marvelous Night For A Moon Dance"
"With The Stars Up Above In Your Eyes"

A Fantabulous Night

And then
We danced wildly

Arms raised to the sky
Feet planted firmly in the clouds

Whirling - Twirling

Wasted

For a fleeting instant
The world seemed pure and brilliant

Finally, I have a sweet taste in my mouth
Couldn't have come soon enough

Luscious

Hell of a night, Gentleman
Hell of a night

Slept well
Only to arise once again to blood, pus, stench and reality

"What A Long Strange Trip It's Been"

FADE TO BLACK

Treated a baby girl today

Third degree burns over twenty-five percent of her tiny body

Utterly tragic
A crippling body blow

As delicately as possible
I debrided this mass of dead skin

She shrieked, and then
She shrieked

That sound
The intensity, the insanity

To be recorded and replayed
And replayed

For the rest of my time

I hear it now
As I speak

It must have felt like the end of the world to this blessed child

I gave her a See's lolly
Chocolate

Pure prevarication
A canard on a stick

Fade to Black

I wanna puke

MY 401K

I'm drinking 8 to 10 liters of water a day
Liters

Can't keep up with this obnoxious, boring heat

One hundred and twenty-five
In the shade

I've peed only six times in a week
Still haven't taken a dump

I'm starting to get concerned

It feels like someone slammed a grapefruit up my ass

My '401K' for a Dulcolax

I'm as thin as a reed
And I know I'm beginning to bend

I look like the Olsen twins
The skinny one

Doesn't matter
I won't break

Not gonna happen
Not now, at least

Too close to the end

Like I said
This was war

Culturally and physically

My most intimate craving
Satisfied

I do believe
You would be proud to share a foxhole with me

Unfortunately
I'll never know if I've won or lost

Pyrrhic at best

Just plugging holes, really
Second year resident stuff

Cut it out
Cut it off

Give it antibiotics

Bobbin' and a weavin'
Shuckin' and a jivin'

Doin' the 'ropa-dope'

Stay steadfast and faithful

Be Here
Right Now

You've probably sensed by this time that prayer is not my scene
Just not in my nature

I'm more of a good vibe guy

Didn't spend thirty years in San Francisco for nothin'

Nevertheless, for whatever reason
I implore something far greater than myself

Please
Oh, Please

Give me the courage
To never forget

"I really did this"

SPENT

Longing to see my love

I wanna be clean again

Haven't taken my scrubs off
For eight days

Can't wait to leave
I wanna stay

Spent
Nothing left

Empty as a pocket

Day 9

4:00 pm

Pried a machete out of a man's skull
I saw his brain

LAST ACT

Back in Nairobi
Leave tonight at 11 pm

Haven't seen a white face all day

So, this is what it feels like
To be a Penguin in Times Square

Need to see the hotel doctor
'STAT'

I'm having a real problem with my belly

Sorry
I'm sorry

"What's that ya say"

The doctor comes in only on Fridays

Oh, Daddy
I am so fucked

Have to make a decision
Now

Either go to the hospital
Or the Other

I choose the Other

Pounded a triple espresso
Waited 20 minutes

Went to my room
Laced up my surgical gloves

Lubricated myself

Liberally

Cover me
Call for back-up

I'm goin' in

Oh, Lordy
The labor was long and tough

No epidural
Au natural

It felt as if I had given birth to a Toyota Prius

At last
At long last

I'm the happiest man in East Africa

This is for 'Z'

Thanks Buddy
'It was a game changer'

ACKNOWLEDGMENTS

Vivian Conan

You made my pages shine
And I love shine

David Chang

If only our world were as beautiful as your vision
Anhedonia be damned

Charles Salzberg

The dude 'du jour' of 63rd Street
Without you, my friend, this volume would not exist
End of story

Elizabeth Graham

Your love and unwavering support are my miracle
Simply stated, you make my life gracious

ABOUT THE AUTHOR

Eli Shaber is a retired surgeon who is now a poet,
traveler, and raconteur.

He lives a quiet, tidy life in New York City
With his wife and puppies.

He can generally be located on his 'STOOP'

www.ingramcontent.com/pod-product-compliance
Lightning Source LLC
Chambersburg PA
CBHW020452100426
42813CB00031B/3334/J